MW00988126

P'TAAH

Jani King

For information address:

Light Source Publishing
PO Box 1251, Joshua Tree, CA 92252 USA
1-760-366-0375

Subscribe to our free email newsletter:
www.ptaah.com

BOOK TITLE:
THE GIFT

AUTHOR:
Jani King

Book and cover design:
Toni Mertin, tmdesigns / Salt Lake City, Utah U.S.A.

If you are unable to order this book from your local bookseller, you may order directly from the publisher. Call 1•888•803•1777

ISBN: 0-9666124-0-X

Printed in the United States of America

Acknowledgments

My love and gratitude to Sy and Mimi Novak, to Alan and Sylvia Rose and to Stefan Hunter, whose loving support made this edition of *The Gift* possible. Thank you, thank you.

Also thanks and love to John Manning, Toni Mertin, Chris Fine and Peter Gorman for your expertise, assistance, and continued loving support.

To my very dear family, Constance, Barry and Murray, as always, thank you for being who you are. To my Marko, thank you.

And finally, this book is dedicated to the memory of our sweet friend Brian Dennis Ferguson.

Jani King.
San Diego, CA 1998

These words are given forth as a gift to you, each one of you; You, who I love absolutely; You, who make my heart sing; You who be a most wondrous aspect of who I AM. These words are simply to remind you of what you really already know.

I will speak to you, in these pages to follow, about fourth density, or ONENESS, and the fact of the Earth and all which exists upon and within Her coming into a collective time of transition. However, be aware that each of you is on your own journey. Each of you is the central sun of your own universe and that the transition is your individual choice, to come to know who you are, NOW.

–P'taah

The Gift

That very tiny fragment of you
which yearns for enlightenment,
which yearns to Come Home, is the very
tiny fragment of you which does not know
that you are already enlightened
and are already At Home within the Divinity
called God-Goddess I AM.

There is really only one question:
Who am I?
There is really only one answer:
I am an extension of the Mind of Creation
experiencing itself in this
dimension of perceived reality.

Know that you create your reality absolutely. Who you are is a grand and multidimensional Master of Creation who creates all the excitement and dramatic scenarios of your life, day by day, simply for the experience of it all. You have co-created the circumstances of your own birthing, your family, your race and socio-economic circumstances. All of this you have created, each lifetime, so that you may garner every experience available to humankind on this plane of reality. The Universe does not judge these experiences however they may be. They simply exist in the IS-NESS of now and in every NOW you may create whatever you desire.

There is an idea within the mind of man
that there are Grand Teachers to come forth
to teach wisdom; to teach you to find
your Divinity. There is also the thought that
you may go forth to other places and other
planets to be taught, in some future time,
how to know who you really are and
how to 'fix' the maladies of your heart.
We tell you no one can teach you. You are
already your own Grand Teacher and are
as divine as you will ever be. If you are looking
to be perfect at some future time,
then it will always be in the future. You only have
the now to know your own perfection.

Unity on your earth may only occur
when you grant equality and validity to
the diversity which exists within your peoples.
This does not mean that you must be
in agreement, or that you should all be the same.
It is to recognize that each person,
each idea is a unique flavor of the Mind of Creation.

As you have perceived yourself to be
separate from the All That Is,
so you have created 'need' to fill the void
of separation. As you allow yourself to recognize
the God-Goddess of you and be filled
with the joy and peace of WHOLENESS,
so you will discover that you have no need at all;
that the outward material and emotional
manifestations of your life will reflect, automatically,
that fullness, without any struggle or strain at all.

Oh my Dear One, how abundant you truly are.
Do you not realise that abundance is not something
you must go out and find? It is who you ARE.
You are not separate from anything. The abundance
of your universe is within you. It IS you.
The glorious expectancy of the dawn, with it's shades of
silver, pink and lavender are yours. The fire of the sunset
is the passion of your life. The song of the birds
which helps the trees to grow is also the song of your soul.
As you gaze out onto your world give fervent thanks
for this abundance which is part of you. As you feel
the joy of abundance fill your heart, how can you not show
forth abundance in your day to day life?
When you are in fear of lack, be still and be filled with
the richness, excitement and abundance of BEING.

Relationships, no matter what kind,
are an outward picture for you to gauge the
relationship you have with aspects of you.
You are not a victim. When your relationships
are not harmonious, when you feel threatened,
diminished, betrayed, not enough, or abandoned,
it is simply that you are in a place of fear. It is time to look
at what you believe about who you are. As you embrace
the fear that you are not worthy of love or
loving, the tenor of your relationships will change,
to reflect the new attitude you have toward yourself.

Fear has come about in your forgetting who you are. You have forgotten that who you really are is an aspect of the God-Goddess expressing Itself, however that may be, in the vibrancy of this reality. There is no such thing as releasing fear, or hiding from it. Fear is valid. There is nothing wrong with fear.

It is the polarity of LOVE. The way to transform fear is to step into it, to embrace it. You may picture fear as the child within you who is terrified of being unworthy of love, joy, abundance and laughter, doomed to abandonment, dying of a broken heart. As you hold the child to your heart, say, "Beloved of my heart, I love you with every part of my being. You are not alone. We live in a safe universe, you and I, and together we are coming home." Thusly, you transform the fear to LOVE.

What is God? Rather you might ask yourself
"What is not God?"
God-Goddess, the Mind of Creation,
the All That Is, you may say, is another description of love
and that is the glue which holds the multiverses together.
Without this energy force, this Light of Creation, there is
no life, no existence. Every cell, every molecule,
every subatomic particle shines with its own God-light.
As you honor who you are as an embodiment
of God-light, how can you not honor everything
and everyone in your universe as a non-separate
part of that same Light?

A Universal Law:
What you resist persists.
This simply means that as you put forth
energy in resistance to the universe,
the universe without judgment, will support you
absolutely and give you more of what you are
putting your energy into.

We say to you that LOVE is simply
another word for God-Goddess.
When you express love to others, you are expressing
the God-Goddess of you. This is immediately
recognized by the others, because it resonates
to their own God-Goddess.
This LOVE is who you all really are.

Your every action, every thought,
every situation
is your own creation.
To deny this truth is to deny
who you are.

Let us speak to you of your pain, my beloved.
Pain is the resistance to a feeling created
from your negative judgment; your judgment of yourself,
your situation and of the co-creators of that situation.
To transmute the pain it is to first take responsibility
for the situation. It is your opportunity to step
into your own God-Goddess-ness.
Then transform the judgment by acknowledging
that it exists, and it exists as a divine tool to show you
WHERE you are and HOW you are NOW.
Once the judgment is dissolved the pain becomes
a neutral feeling. Be still. Be in the allowance.
Give forth the thanks for this opportunity to BE
the more of who you really are.
Ah, Beloved, now you KNOW you are truly
not separate from the All That Is.

You have created yourself here and now
to take part in the transformation of your world.
This transformation is a shift in consciousness
not only of humanity, but of the planet Herself and
everything upon and within Her.
Sometimes you become afraid that in this shift
you will lose those who are dear to you
who are perhaps not as consciously aware as you.
Beloved, we would remind you that this
change is about LOVE, and love is non-separation.
You will lose nothing and no one.

Your mission in life is simply to come to know
who you really are. Everything else is a game wherein
you may monitor your own progress.
There is nothing to DO. You exist in your absolute
perfection every now moment. You are an exquisite jewel
of creation NOW, not when you have changed all of
the parts of you that you judge to be unworthy and unlovable.
You want to do great deeds, to be of grand service
to humanity, but we tell you that the greatest service is
to come into the realization that simply by BEING in
the love and honor of who you really are,
you change the consciousness of all humanity.
Thusly, you will light up your world.
Can there be a greater service?

The diversity of teachings in your world are
understandably sometimes quite confusing for you.
There are so many stories of light entities and
dark entities; implants and conspiracies,
rites and rituals, do's and don'ts.
There are stories about the evils of man which you
must atone for and methodologies to which you must
adhere in order to become enlightened.
The list could go on and on. However, the truth is
that you are your own power-sourceness.
You are a sovereign being. The enlightenment you seek
is already within you, as is the knowledge of
the multiverses. If you want to give your power away
then it is your sovereign right to do so.
You have been doing it for eons. If anyone tells you
"You can only do it this way," bless them and turn away.
If what anyone tells you is fearbased, or in any way
limited or limiting, bless them and turn away.

There is no judgment in the universe apart from
that judgment you have about yourself.
Every time you sit in judgment of anyone or anything
outside yourself, it is really you whom you judge.
There will never be a time when you are called to
a higher judgment. Very often in your day-by-day life
you find yourself in judgment, then judge the judgment.
What a double bind! Well, that is alright.
Just remind yourself that judgment itself is an attribute
of divinity. It is your yardstick. It is your monitor,
by which you may gauge your own beliefs
and fears in that now moment.
Give thanks for this. From the judgment you may grow.

Beloved, your longing for the fourth dimension,
or ascension, or any reality apart from this,
is simply the measure of your dissatisfaction
with the NOW. Until you can come to the joy and
fulfillment of this life, loving your exquisite planet,
healing the anguished heart, aligning the fears that keep
you imprisoned, living in the excitement and fullness
of each moment without a past or a future,
this dimension is all you can know. There is no escape.
That is the dichotomy: As you live in the joy and harmony
of this life experience without desiring any other,
you automatically create the space to experience that
expanded reality called fourth density,
called ascension, called ONE-NESS.

All of humanity was star-seeded.
Many of you are quite comfortable with that knowing at this time. Indeed, many of you feel that you are not 'at home' on this planet and feel a longing to return from whence you came. Some of you consult seers and teachers to find out where 'home' really is.
I will tell you, home is the place within you that knows itself to be in non-separation from anyone anywhere.
It does not matter where you are from; it is not important.
It will not help you. It is another diversion to keep you away from feeling, from examining your beliefs and fears.
You have created yourselves here in this time and place to become all that you can be in this reality.
There is nothing else.

Your ego was designed to be the sensor
of exterior life. You cannot get rid of it or sublimate it.
Indeed, as you try to do so, the old law of
the universe which is stated 'What you resist persists'
will bring the ego into a stronger and stronger position.
Your ego is a most valuable aspect of you.
It is merely to bring it into balance. When you find yourself
heartily in defense of yourself, know that the ego is in fear
of the judgment of others. Be still.
Go to the fear and embrace the child within you
who is afraid. Also, it is to remind yourself that
what anyone thinks of you is none of your business.

Life IS meant to be easy.
Your life is meant to be of love and laughter,
abundance and fulfillment. What keeps you from
these things is your belief about reality,
the fear that you are not worthy and all of the old emotional
baggage you carry. Every time you find yourself in a struggle
you are in a place of fear. Each time you refuse to
deal with an emotional issue in the now moment you are
simply adding to the emotional baggage. If you will not
examine your belief structures and fears and deal with
the emotions, you limit yourself to a most confining prison.
Each NOW is another opportunity for you
to choose how it may be for you.

The preoccupation with what is right or wrong for you to eat is not necessary. Your health is not dependent upon it. That which is the beingness of flora and fauna, in a way, is co-created by you and the flora and fauna, for your nourishment, both physical and spiritual. The nourishment is gained by your giving forth thanks for what is provided, to the Spirit of that which is ingested. In the opening of your heart and giving thanks, you cause the enlightenment of the food... the enlightenment of the spiritual "body" of the food, and in the giving forth of thanks you are also creating the enlightenment of your physical structure.

Dear One, forgiveness is a concept of limitation. Does this sound strange to you? Well you see, in the broader sense of things, no one ever 'did' anything to you. You create your own reality absolutely. Everything in your life you have created, or rather co-created and have done so for your greatest spiritual growth, whether or not you accept it as such. You are not a powerless victim. You really have the hardest time in the negative judgment and 'forgiveness' of yourself. Understand that every situation is a learning process for the benefit of all peoples concerned, to help you to grow in love, honor, sovereignty and compassion.

The natural inclination of your consciousness is to
turn toward the spiritual truths which
reflect the Divinity you really are.
The natural inclination of your physical body is to shine
forth with radiant health, reflecting the Divinity
which is the life force within every cell.
Every part of you yearns to bask in the light of that Divinity,
called love, in the same fashion that a flower turns
irresistibly to the light of the sun.

There is no such thing as extraneous creation,
or parts of creation that should not be,
or do not fit in to your reality.
If something exists it is as valid as anything else,
or it would have no existence.

Guilt, Beloved One, is simply a lesson not learned.
Everything not created out of love is created out of
fear of the belief in your own lack or unworthyness,
and every such situation is co-created to reflect the fears
and beliefs of the co-creators also, so that all participants
may grow. You have always done the best you could
in the only way you knew how. There is no judgment.
As you come into this more unlimited way of thinking,
as you come to embrace the fears,
align the judgments and transmute the pain,
you will find that the guilt will simply fade away.
You will not need to repeat the lesson!

You have a most amusing saying in your world:
"Time is what stops everything occurring at once."
This is valid. You may say that when you are birthed,
you are birthed into a time-lock, and what you experience
in that time-lock are the separate events called life.
You may say that time is a referencing point.
Then you experience what you call death
and after a period of other-reality experience
you may choose to come back to this reality,
in another time-lock for yet another 'life.'
However, in a more expanded sense,
time is simply an illusion.
Outside of this space-time continuum
all of the lifetimes occur simultaneously,
each in its own glorious NOW.

It simply does not matter who you were in your past lives,
nor what glorious or terrible deeds you performed,
nor with whom. The only importance in your life is NOW.
It does not matter what occurred in your life yesterday
or last year. Whatever has occurred which
is not aligned will be presented to you and re-presented
continually until you do align it.
It does not even matter what the 'story'
of external events consists of. You will notice that
what will be recurring, no matter what the story,
will be the same FEELING. As you go to the feeling,
in allowance and embracement of the fears,
in the NOW moment, you effect the change into alignment,
not only in this life, but in what you call your past
and your future lives, as all of the lifetimes
are occurring simultaneously.

Love is the Alpha and Omega of your life.
Without it you cannot survive.
Love is what fills the empty space within you.
As you become filled with the love of who you are,
in the knowing that you are an aspect of the God-Goddess,
so you radiate that love to all about you.
From this place of being, all that you will be able to perceive
will be the reflection of that love shining back at you.
Oh my Beloved, what wondrousness, indeed!

It is time for you to learn to listen to the knowing within you. When you find yourself in a muddle, simply be still and ask from the God-Goddess of your own being, to allow the wisdom and knowing to float into your consciousness. Sometimes you invalidate your knowing because the answers do not seem to make sense to you, or indeed the answer is not the one the ego wants to hear. It is to remember that your logical conscious mind is most often not aware of the larger scheme of things, whereas the greater part of who you are knows all of the probabilities, and indeed, knows that which will be of most benefit to you.

We say to you "Go forth and do what makes your heart sing." Please note that we do say 'heart,' not 'ego.' You will find that simply to gratify the ego will not bring you the fulfillment you desire, nor fill the emptiness within you. Sometimes it is difficult for you to know the difference between heart and ego. That which is of the heart is that which is of benefit to all peoples concerned in a decision. How do you know what is benefit when you do not have an overview? Simply be still and ask yourself, then listen to the feeling. The feeling of peace and comfort is your answer.

Angels and Guides are valid.
However, know that the greater spiritual beingness of you
occupies all of the dimensions simultaneously.
At another level you are also Angels and Guides.
Therefore, we say to you it is of utmost benefit if you will
understand that it is, in that place of non-separation,
all part of your own soul energy.
Instead of calling on an outside authority,
call upon the unlimited, eternal I AM.
In this fashion you strengthen your own power sourceness.

Simplicity, Dear One, that is the key.
Keep it Simple! There is nothing outside of you
but a mirror. Go to the feeling.
If you feel joyous then go with the flow of it.
If it is not harmonious, be still.
Examine the beliefs you have about the situation.
Embrace the fear and transmute the pain.
Everything else is just a story.

As you grow in awareness and expand
your consciousness you will find that your view of
your world also expands. As you view the dramas
and pain and anguish of your brothers and sisters
it is important that you balance that which is detachment
and compassion. It is to be in that place of support,
open heartedness and unconditional love.
To show forth tenderness and giving of yourself,
without becoming hooked into the story,
without reinforcing feelings of
victimhood or powerlessness.

Know, my Beloved, that never in your life have you
made a wrong decision or choice.
Everything that you have ever done has brought you
to this place, this NOW of new knowledge,
new choice points and new opportunity.
You have never been, nor will you be, judged and
condemned for anything you have done.
Everything is simply a learning experience for you
to come to the knowing that you are God-Goddess
made manifest in this your perceived reality;
to come from separateness to ONE-NESS
in this perfect and eternal NOW.

Self honesty is a tool without which you will find it very difficult to grow. Without it, you find that you disguise and dress up the reasons for your actions and reactions. It is part of your fear that you are not worthy and fear of judgment by others; in other words, having to be 'seen to be' more than you think you are. By being honest with yourself you have the most wonderful tool to discover your secret fears and hidden beliefs about yourself and your reality. In the embracement of those fears you become centered and strong.

This is called sovereignty, from whence comes your creative choice points, to grow into your own power.

To be honest with others about who you are,
to speak your truth, is to be vulnerable.
We say to you that vulnerability is a most powerful place of being. It is that place where there can be no dissension.
It is also the most fearful place for many of you,
because you fear judgment.
You fear that if you open your heart,
someone will put a knife in it. The reality is that when you speak forth your truth you are really allowing the merging of hearts to take place because vulnerability is irresistible. When you find that there is truly nothing to defend, your ego has taken a back seat and your heart is driving you to a place of non-separation.

Honor who you are and in the doing
you cannot but honor every aspect of Creation.
What does that mean, really? It is simply that as you
come to know that who you are is a spark
of Divine Creation you feel awe in the wondrousness,
immensity and power of you. In the recognition of the
pure potential of what it is to be a human aspect of
The All That Is, you are enflamed with love of you
and able to access that flame of Divinity not only
within yourself, but within every unique aspect of
Creation perceived in your reality. You honor who you are
by the allowance of BEING that unique aspect of
Creation that you are, without judgment.
You honor all life in the same way.

You ask about trust, Dear One.
Well, think about how you trust yourself.
How much do you trust that you are an eternal,
unlimited Being who has the knowledge of
the multiverses within you? How much do you trust
that whatever experiences you bring forth
are opportunities for you to expand into the Light;
that the greater part of who you are,
with the universe, supports and nourishes you
absolutely, if you will allow it.
When you trust your own Beingness
the question of trusting others does not arise.

You ask me, "How can I trust?"
We say to you that you have unlimited trust,
which you experience every day of your life.
You trust that the sun will rise each day.
Trust is what creates your reality.
Doubt is your trust that the outcome
will be negative.
You may change that belief.

Laughter, Precious Being, that is the great aligner! As you allow the joy and the laughter to bubble forth, there is no judgment, no fear, no limited beliefs. In those moments of great laughter you are truly in the NOW, without past and without future, but simply in the eternal NOW, in joy and alignment with your universe. In that moment, your brain releases the healing chemicals which allow your body to reflect this unity in the manner of health and well being.

The beauty which surrounds you is
an exquisite mirror for you to know how beautiful
you really are. When you acknowledge beauty
it is to know that if you were not beauty,
how could you perceive it outside of you?
Do you judge the beauty of nature? No!
It is all beautiful to you in myriad different ways.
You do not compare the beauty of a sunset
to the beauty of a blossom and say one is more
beautiful than another. In the same fashion
do not compare yourself with anyone else.
Each one of you is awesomely beauteous in your own
unique and divine fashion. Without you, Beloved,
the universes would not be the same.

From your belief structures about reality
you see that everything in your life is good-bad,
positive-negative, happy-sad and so on.
We say to you very often that all of this dimension may be
perceived as polarity. However, be aware that polarity
is an illusion. What affects transformation is
the transcending of that illusion of polarity.
Your beliefs may be likened unto the house that you live in,
which is very often a very tiny box which gives you
no room to stretch and grow. As you come to know that
this illusion called life, called polarity, called limitation,
is self-imposed, then by the simple act of choice
you may transcend it, to become limitless and sovereign.

Take time each day for yourself.
As you get caught up in the idea of 'duty,'
'no time,' 'must succeed' and that anything
which is pleasurable just for you, must be selfish,
self indulgent or not deserved, remind yourself
that the very fact that you exist makes you worthy
of all the wondrousness that you can imagine, and more.
By taking time each day for you to harmonize
and balance yourself, you are honoring
and nurturing yourself, which enables you to
be more creative, joyous and of greater service
to humanity in your day to day life.

Beloved, we suggest to you that you learn
to become a creative detective,
as in your books of fiction. By learning the reasons
for your reactive behavioral patterns
you can effect the changes that you desire in your life.
One of the maladies that beset you in your day to days
is what you term stress. What is stress?
It is a manifestation of fear.
It is fear of an imagined outcome, which most often
in your world means failure. When you find yourself
in stress or struggle, be still and ask yourself
"What am I afraid of here? What outcome am I attached to?"
You will be most surprised as you uncover beliefs
that you did not realize you held and which really
no longer serve you. Also, perhaps, how attached
you are to what other people think of you.

CHOICE!

You exercise it thousands of times each day
without even realizing you are doing so.
Be aware of how you choose.
If you are going to do it, you might as well
choose joy and peace and harmony.

If you are going to wait until
everything is 'fixed' before you will
allow yourself to feel freedom and happiness,
be prepared for a short and miserable life!
Do not wait.
Your freedom and happiness are a choice NOW.

Everything in your world is valid,
else it would not exist.
Everything has a purpose for the higher good.
Even that which you would judge to be
most destructive upon your plane may serve you,
if you will allow it.

Keep it Simple.
Whatever the drama is, whatever the story,
come back to the feeling.

Allow yourself to dream the impossible dream.
Allow your imagination to run wild.
Be who you are in this moment.
Thrill yourself with spontaneous action
and be the child again.
Be practical. Plan for a miracle.
Ah! What excitement, Beloved.

Being of service to others may be a smile,
a loving word or support when it is least expected.
Being of service to others is simply to make
a gift of who you are, to another.
BE the gift
every day of your life.

Dear One, you are a miracle of this universe.
Acknowledge that you are, and look about
you to see the miracles reflected back to you.
Allow the wonderment of these miracles
to permeate your being.
This wonderment is, indeed, life-renewing
and life-affirming and absolutely
life-prolonging.

No one and no-thing
can fill the empty space within you,
except you.

As you are living in the focus of NOW,
without a past and without a future,
you are allowing the space for new knowledge
and solutions to 'problems' to float
into your consciousness
without striving and struggling.

There is no place on your earth which is
more sacred than another.
The place you are at this moment, on your earth,
is where you are supposed to be, until the excitement
or desire of the heart will move you to another.
Know that you live in a safe universe.
No place is unsafe, really. Safety is within you,
in the knowing that you are safe
and the universe supports that knowing absolutely.

You are more than your intelligence,
more than your body, more than your passions,
more than your fears. If you are ruled by any one
or more of these, understand that it is a choice.
What is part of your soul energy is WILL.
You may choose to be the MORE of you
and as you exercise this WILL to BE the more,
the universe, or God-Goddess energy,
supports that choice.

You have never made a wrong decision,
my beloved, and you never will.
The effect of any decision is simply
a learning experience,
however you may judge it.

The macrocosmic universes are what you
may term the galaxies.
Microcosmic universes or galaxies are contained
within your own physical structure.
The mathematical dimensions are identical.
How is that for a miracle?

Freedom is in the knowing that
in every moment you have a choice.
Limitation is in
the not exercising that choice.

The intellectual understanding of the concepts
we give forth to you are not enough
to change your life.
However, using that understanding
to RECOGNIZE THE FEELING,
to access your heart,
will turn your life around immediately.

When something wondrous occurs in your life, look in the mirror and say, "I have created this. I, this grand and multi-dimensional being have created this."

Fourth density, transcendence or
enlightenment, or whatever you may call it,
is not issued forth as a panacea
for the ills of your time.
It is simply the result of your embracement
of every facet of who you are.

As you are focusing on 'have not,'
you are not focusing on 'have.'
Whatever you put your focus or energy into
is what you will draw to you.

You have an idea of perfection as being
a 'finished' product and that when you are perfect
you will be a 'finished' article, so to speak.
We say to you there is no finish, no end.
Who you are at this moment, in this now,
is the perfection of the Mind of Creation
unfolding unto infinity.

In your world of polarity you are
very concerned with what you term
'profit and loss, win or lose'.
Know, however, that as you come into
the knowing that you may create
whatever you desire, without 'need' or desperation,
every transaction may be one of win-win
with profit to all, without loss.

As you become more attuned,
more in the knowing that you are separate
from nothing and no one,
you will find that the moments of illumination
become longer and longer, until there will be no time
when you do not know that you are truly
an expression of the God-Goddess.

When you find yourself in a muddle,
ask yourself "How would I deal with this if
I were an enlightened one?"
Thusly, you allow yourself to tap into
the SELF of you who IS an enlightened being
and allow that knowing to issue forth.

Vulnerability is one of the most powerful
attributes of you. Realize that if two people
come together and one is vulnerable
there can be no confrontation.
What is vulnerability?
It is to speak your truth, to open your heart
and say, "This is who I am and
this is what frightens me."

When you find yourself struggling to manipulate
and control external events in your life,
look at the fear which lies beneath these actions.
If you would simply give up and allow the flow of events,
stating your preferred outcome,
you would find that the result will be exactly
as you desired, without the struggle.

Love or fear, it is your choice in any moment
how you perceive it, how you live it.
You may cower in your fear or dance in the light.
The time will come when you will be very bored with living
in the fear, being paralyzed in a no-life.
One day you will open your eyes and say,
"This day I will step into the Light".

Every time you require a definition you acquire a limitation.

The changes which are occurring,
heralding the transition of the earth and of humanity
need not be chaotic. As you step further and further
into the expansion of consciousness, so you become
more anchored in who you are. You will not be tossed
as a leaf in the wind, feeling powerless and out of control.
Rather you will be in joyous celebration
of the changes, garnering the wisdom
and living in the Light of you.

When you find yourself in defense
of other peoples opinions of you,
it is your Ego defending itself.
When you say, "but I...," it is
your Ego defense mechanism kicking in.
That is alright. Embrace your Ego.
It is frightened of being dispossessed.

Imagine that there is a string of light from your heart
which connects you to every other human upon your plane.
Now imagine many strings of light which connect you
to every tree, blade of grass, insect and animal.
From your crown, see a golden thread which goes forth
to the stars, connecting you to every being
on every planet of the universes and all the dimensions.
Let that feeling resonate in your heart,
so you will know how it is to be in non-separation.

You are loved and cherished
on every dimension.
The names and numbers do not matter.
They do not mean anything to you.
What is meaningful to you is your own heart,
your own soul, your own consciousness,
your own potential, your own divine beauty.
However, we desire you to know
you are not alone.

Who you are is unlimited potential.
Who you are is a powerhouse, NOW. Everything that
has been in your past is who you are NOW.
It is alright. YOU are ALRIGHT.
You are everything you can possibly be at this moment.
You are glorious, and when you can accept that you are,
think of the tomorrows you will create!

Enlightenment is not about being good.
It is about BEING.

What you invalidate, indeed,
you empower.

As you label conscious, sub-conscious, un-conscious, super-conscious, persona, body, spirit, soul and God, you are compartmentalizing and separating all the glorious parts of who you are. That is alright, but know that you really are an homogenized body of wondrous energy, of Divinity experiencing being human in this NOW.

When you can imagine that the
All-That-Is has no personification,
as such, then you may
truly see the All-That-Is in everything,
including who you are.

That which you term religion, upon your plane,
has nothing to do with the Spiritual truths of the universes,
which require no rites, rules or rituals.
It is that which is a tool of enslavement to keep you
in chains, to keep you in control that you may not
know sovereignty and free dominion.
It is valid. You have created it.
But it is not necessary for your enlightenment.

Dear One, you are every facet of
every being ever to walk this planet, and more.
You create every lifetime to garner
every human experience,
and it is all a grand illusion.

Whatever you use as power-tools,
crystals and suchlike, are valid.
However, know that you are your own
power-sourceness and you need no outside tools
for your inside enlightenment.

Every situation has within it
a pearl of wisdom for you, if you will allow it.
To harvest the pearls is to adorn yourself
with celestial jewels, to drape yourself in robes
of celestial light and to grow wings with
which to fly into the arms of eternal bliss.

Until you can embrace and enjoy
all the facets of who you are, you are not whole.
When you are whole, it is called coming home.
There are wondrous beings, who love you absolutely,
who have planned a glorious surprise party
in celebration of your return!

There is no such thing as death. When you become tired of wearing one color every day of your life, it is a joy to take off that suit of clothing. Your body, you may say, is a suit of clothing. When you take off that clothing you do not cease to be the wondrous jewel you are.

Sometimes when you are in a bit of a pickle,
you ask of the universe,
"Please send forth an answer to me,"
and you sit and wait to hear celestial voices.
Well, most often the answer is not in the form of
a celestial voice, but in something quite mundane
in your day to day life. If you are aware,
you will see that you have created the answer
in the most tangible and irrefutable fashion.
When you have the expectation that the answers
may only occur in such and such a way,
you have closed down all other possibilities for wisdom.

Know that in the appearance of more war,
more violence, more discord,
you are seeing the polarity of more love,
more joy, more harmony.
The Love will embrace the fear and create Light.
As it is within you, so it is without.

This life is about BEING,
human BEING, however it is,
with all its joys and all its sorrows.
Feel how exquisite it is, your tempestuous path
to enlightenment. You chose it. You love it.
If you did not, it would not BE
and that is the wondrous and very humorous
dichotomy of it.

When we speak of beings of 'higher dimension',
we are speaking of the rate of vibratory frequency,
not as 'better than' or 'more important' than humanity.
There is no being anywhere who is more than another.
The angel is not more than the human.
The angel simply knows the 'MORE' of who it is.
You are still learning.
There is no hierarchy within Divinity.

You are a sexual being, from your birthing to your transition, however you may express it. When you look at how sex is used as a tool of manipulation or control, and embrace your fears and judgments around your sexuality, then truly, sexuality may indeed become a most joyous expression of the heart; an integrated facet of your own God-Goddessness. Your sexual expression is no different than any other outward expression of who you are.

Every action, every decision you have ever made
has brought you to this place, this now.
Bless all that has happened in your life
which has been discordant. You have created it all
that you may know who you really are.
Own it all. You are not a victim,
and neither is anyone else.

When you embrace all the things
about yourself that you find unlovable,
you have automatically allowed the space
for its opposite trait to manifest.

If you find yourself impatient and cross
because something you fervently desired
is not made manifest, be still and check any fear,
belief, or expectation which may be impeding
the manifestation. If you feel clear about that,
then simply know that the greater part of who
you are has something much grander than what
you have envisioned lined up for you
in the ripeness of time. Allow it.

It is impossible to change the expression
of Divinity that you are.
You may simply acknowledge who you are, or not.
That is your choice.

Life is what is occurring whilst you are very busy planning your future and regretting your past.

Whatever you desire to manifest,
simply put it forth to the universe and KNOW
that it already IS. The moment you decide
that what you may desire can only occur 'this way.'
in 'this timing,' you are shutting down
your own creativity and millions of possibilities.
It is wonderful to make plans, but it is not to be rigid.
It is to allow the flow of creativity, that everything
may flow from your own Divinity. Indeed.

Doubt is of the intellect.
Knowing is of feeling.
If there is doubt, there is not the knowing.
Knowing contains no doubt at all.

When your hearts are quickened
with excitement and joy, every cell in your body
resonates to that. In the cellular structure of your body,
every cell ,EVERY cell has its own consciousness,
its own integrity, its own joyous impetus of creativity.
In this fashion, diseasement is not something you catch
like a stray dog. The diseasement of your body,
indeed, is a reflection of the diseasement of your heart.

Each time, by word or deed,
you invalidate yourself,
you will create situations which
support that invalidation.

You are so afraid to feel your feelings,
in the belief that you will die of the pain of it.
The truth is, you will die if
you do NOT go to the feeling.

For eons of time mankind has been living
a dream called reality.
It is your destiny to awake from the dream
into the REALITY of DIVINTY.
Now is the time.

Those who would control you are
those who are afraid they have no control.
Those who lust after power
are those who fear powerlessness.
Those who would steal are in fear of lack.
Those who would torment and torture
are those who, indeed, are tortured and tormented.
Beloved, have compassion for their fear.
As you may, without judgment, enfold these ones
into your heart, indeed you will change the reality.

You may create the transition as you would
desire it: with love and joy and exuberance,
in wild creativity, with great honor and integrity.
The words you have will not describe the
ecstatic explosion, nor can you imagine how you will
all be in that time, when every atom and molecule
upon this planet, and the whole planet herself
will radiate with divine light.
Such exquisite beauty is beyond imaginings.

The external situations in your life
have no meaning in and of themselves.
It is you, your consciousness which designates
a meaning. If you designate a negative meaning,
the result is negative.
By designating a positive meaning,
the result is positive,
thusly allowing for expansion.

You think that when you come
to enlightenment it is the end of it all.
It is only the beginning.

The Self that you really are is more than
your waking or sleeping self, more than
the emotions you experience
in your day-to-days.
Next time you are angry, be still and ask yourself,
"Who is angry?" The next time you are frustrated,
or unhappy, be still and ask yourself,
"Who is frustrated?,"
"Who is unhappy?" Just be still and listen.
Feel the SELF of you. This SELF is not angry,
frustrated or unhappy.

Each time you invalidate anybody else,
you are invalidating who you are.
As you invalidate yourself you are not
allowing yourself to be who you are,
and you are disallowing your
own potential for expansion.

You are the orchestrator of your own life.
You are the composer and the conductor and all of
the instruments in this grand orchestra.
You may create wonderful symphonies.
We suggest that you become fascinated with the
beauteous music you create, so that all of your life
you may show forth the harmony of it.

In the changes which are occurring
upon your planet and in the transitions to come
there are many of humanity, among what you would
term the power brokers of your world, who are plotting
their own power base. In truth, they are working very well
to accomplish that which is completely
unbeknown to them. It is called
"God moves in mysterious ways." Indeed!

Your soul has no gender.
It is not even human.
Allow yourself to contemplate this,
in all its non-limitation.

That which you regard as something
very important in your life and to which you
devote much energy to create,
takes no more energy than that which you regard
to be quite insignificant and create without
thinking about. Is this food for thought?

You cannot change what you do not
acknowledge and own.
Acknowledge and own the beliefs and fears
and self-invalidations which keep you from
the truth of who you really are.

Everything in physical existence is simply
coalesced energy which vibrates at its own frequency.
You have your own unique frequency,
different to anyone else's.
The frequency of humanity is different to
the frequency of a cow or a piece of furniture.
It is by these frequencies that you perceive differentiation.
In truth, energy is energy, and energy is of the Source.

There is nothing to do, nothing to fix.
It is simply to allow yourself to be excited by the
idea that you exist in this reality enveloped
in the tender arms of the
Perfect and Divine Self of you,
who is simply an extension of
the SOURCE.

Dear One, we ask you to contemplate this:
Love which is egobased has somewhat
of a feeling of fear, of possession, or even entrapment
attached to it. Love in the real sense
has no thought of giving or receiving
attached to it at all. Love simply extends itself,
unmindful of anything else.
Love simply IS.
Love is also simply who you really are.

The state of health or diseasement of your physical body is simply a mirror of your emotional state of being. One is as valid as the other. The universe does not judge one as being better or worse than the other. Your body's desire at cellular level is to show forth radiant wholeness and as you heal and align your emotional body, so your physical body will automatically reflect that change.

Allow the children of your world to grow with the knowledge of their own power. Tell them they create their own reality, and how they do that. Allow them to know there is no such thing as 'success versus failure.' Encourage that which is their dreams, and tell them that by their dreams and their imagination, they create what they desire. Teach them cooperative play rather than competition. Honor their sovereignty and love them absolutely in the knowledge they are Gods and Goddesses come forth to be your teachers and mirrors.

If you were to stand aside from what you term to be your 'real life,' you would know that in a manner of speaking, your 'dream life' is more real than your waking reality. In your dream state you commune with other aspects of you; with dear friends and companions not of this reality, and indeed, those who are. Oftentimes you play and adventure in other dimensions and with beings you would regard to be extra-terrestrial. Understand that these communications are initiated by you, for your own expansion, even when you can bring forth no conscious remembrance. If you would desire to remember, simply ask forth before you sleep. However, know that many of these journeyings do not fit into the limited boxes of your definition of reality.

You have control of your life
by letting go the NEED to control it.
Let go, and let GOD, GODDESS,
I AM.

You are ALREADY the fourth density
being you desire to be.
You are ALREADY tapping into
that higher consciousness you think is so elusive.
You are ALREADY growing into the expansion
of who you really are.
As you believe it, so it is.
You are what you believe you are.

The measure with which you base your feelings
of love, joy, validation and success on
other people and external events,
is the measure with which you are bound
to feel rejection, unhappiness,
invalidation and failure.

There has existed and still does, in a fashion, a belief that your bodies may be 'taken over' by what is termed to be 'evil spirits.' We remind you that you are sovereign beings and not ever victims. That which is termed evil is that which is the manifestation of fear, unembraced.

What you regard to be senility is
the gradual relinquishing of the present and the desire
to be gone from this place and time.
This signifies the loosening of the ties between
consciousness and body and the consciousness spending
more and more time out of the body
to experience adventures of another kind.

Hating conflict and violence
will not bring harmony and peace.
Loving harmony and peace brings
harmony and peace.

Love is who you are.
Love is the true description of your SELF
as the thought of the Mind of Creation.
All else is an illusion,
a misperception of the limited
ego-consciousness.

It is not external events which are your lessons.
The wisdom comes from the recognition
of the FEELINGS attached to those events.
That the lessons you bring to yourself are often
unpleasant or discordant is simply your mind-set of eons
of time which tells you that as a guilty
and unworthy person, you deserve nothing better.

Look at how often each day you turn your focus
to that which you perceive to be the differences
and conflicts within yourself and between you
and your brothers and sisters.
When you will turn your focus to the unity,
to the exemplification of Divinity that you share,
then you will close that perceived gap
called separation.

The desire to manifest which comes out of
a place of fear or need, does not support
the most fervent desire of your heart,
which is to come to know the I Am who needs
nothing and may have anything,
simply for the joy of it.

We give forth words to you, and in a way,
these words create separation. Your logical mind
interprets the words according to your own limited
perceptions, fears and beliefs. We would ask you to go
to the feeling the words generate within you.
Thereby you may know your truth of them.

It is not necessary to go back into the past
to align that which has created pain and anguish,
or indeed, to create the healing of your physical body.
It is only necessary in this now moment to embrace
the thought that you are a Divine and Perfect Expression
of Creation. In that thought, you are automatically
in that place of responsibility, non-judgment and
allowance of the feeling which that thought engenders.

Other peoples idea of who you are
and who you should be usually have nothing
to do with the Truth of your Being.
You can buy into the limitation
of these ideas or not.

There has always been somewhat of a fear
within you of the unknown quality of limitlessness,
of having no boundaries, of being infinite.
However, we assure you that just as what you have
already expanded into has now become quite familiar,
so it will continue in this fashion.
You truly have no limit and the Self of you
is very comfortable with its own infinite Divinity.

Beloved, we ask you to look at how you
all identify with roles. The role of son or daughter,
mother or father, husband or wife, employer or employee.
Understand how you limit yourself by these ideas.
It is time now to step beyond the roles
that you have been assigned and those you have
assigned to other people in your life.
Be aware of how your ideas
of these roles limit your relationships
and keep you in chains.

The process of 'becoming' enlightened
is really a concept of ego-consciousness.
The truth is, you are already as perfect and Divine
as you are ever going to be. It is simply that that fact
is not recognized by the ego-consciousness.
Will you remind yourself of this when you fall into
the dismals about your 'progress'?

As you allow yourself to reveal who
you are to those about you, so this allowance
will help heal the wounds
of your heart. As you reveal yourself,
so the judgments and fears about yourself
are on the way to being aligned.
You only fear revelation because you think
that the secret truth is that you are less than
you should be, and that the real you
is absolutely unlovable.
How strange it is that all of the secret fears
of humanity are exactly the same!

Beloved, the Truth of how you may manifest joy and harmony and abundance in your life is simple. However, as you get caught up in the seeming complexity of your day to day life, be aware that it is your mind-set which creates the complexity. You have a choice to continue in this mind-set, or to be still and look at HOW you create it and how you may change it.

In this timing, in your society, many of you are feeling the stirring to do something different; to change the pattern of your life. Most of you have been programmed to think that once you have made a choice as to what your 'life's work' is, then it would be considered flighty, or fickle, to change it. Also there enters in an element of fear around security. We remind you that nothing is cast in stone, nor are any of the mulitudinous choices mutually exclusive. It does not have to be 'this' OR 'this' for the rest of your days. It can be this AND this AND this AND this. You really are grandly creative, Beloved. You can do any thing you want. Go for it! Follow your excitement! Do what makes your heart sing!

It is most beneficial for you not
to focus on that which you think must be 'fixed'
before you can step into 'enlightenment.'
As we have said many times to you,
there is nothing to fix and whatever you focus on
you draw to you. It is rather to focus on
the joy of being God-Goddess
smelling the rose NOW.

The excitement and the singing of the heart
which you experience when you contemplate
an imagined joyous action is the indication
of the very real expression of who you are.
When you deny the action, you deny yourself
the gift of yourself, to yourself
and to your world.

Your life is not meant to be serious,
my Beloved. How long is it since you
have allowed yourself lightheartedness and laughter?
All of this business is about enLIGHTenment,
not enHEAVYment.

You know, you really are so wonderful.
You are amazing, astonishingly beautiful
and astonishingly courageous.
We understand that most of the time
you cannot acknowledge this to be so.
However beloved, as you expand
and reveal the YOU of you to yourself,
you will see YOU with my eyes.
How is that for a tongue twister?
I salute you and love you absolutely.

I thank you for sharing who you are with that which be I.
As you are reading the words we have issued forth,
the essence of You mingles with the essence that I AM
in an ecstatic dance called Light, called Love.
We desire only to serve you, that you may recognize
the perfume of your own blossoming.

It is now time for you to dwell in
the House of eternal LOVE
and play in the garden called heaven
on the earth of your own creation.
We are waiting for you.